Individualism

Natasha Nand

BookLeaf
Publishing

India | USA | UK

Presentation by *BookLeaf Publishing*

Web: www.bookleafpub.com

E-mail: info@bookleafpub.com

ISBN : 9789357448666

First edition 2021

Morals

Go with the flow;
challenge what you know.
Hold your breath,
dive down low.

Fight for your ground
for truth cannot be found.
If you stub your toe
the embarrassment will be profound.

It bubbles and burns
and makes your stomach churn
to know your true foe
and see the fates turn.

Inhale and suck a breath,
gusto wards off the sorrow of death.
There's no need to be stern
for we are all and one flesh.

Refusal of Change

Around and around we go
A record player with a tone so low
Spin, spin, and squeak on repeat
An album of sorrow and pain and defeat.

Around and around we go
They said together we would glow
The needle bumps on the turn
As I continue to wait for your return.

Around and around we went
Our time I once thought was well spent.
The music still flows to my ears…
No more does it turn my gears.

Around and around we went
You misinterpreted what I meant
The turntable was smashed
It was not much longer before we crashed.

The record creaks as it halts,
ending its lifetime by default.
For now we must say goodbye
But still, I cannot help but cry.

Reaching the Goal

Open your eyes
And let your flesh dry;
I want to show you the world
And hold you up to the sky

Let yourself blossom,
Hide not like a possum.
The world gives its judgement
They are only solemn.

Give up now your hearts
For we will not part
Instead remember us
Our lives were a work of art.

Rise and pull from the globe
Take your own time to load
For the world lies ahead
And does its best to corrode.

The Spear to the Heart

I gave you too many chances
Not once did you learn my name
Yet always you accepted blame

One chance
And you forgot that we were one
Forgot all the times we had fun

Two chances
And you didn't care about the fights
Only cared instead about the next flight

Three Chances
And I began to break down
With you not caring that I would drown

A million more to go
Only for me to give up
With tears filling up only a single cup

But it will be ok
A broken heart will always mend

But the memories keep playing with no end.

5

Fear

Run, race to the edge

Everyone, everything
they come bearing arms

Arms of sharp steel,
words tipped with poison,
silence cut with gasoline

Fingers scraping your throat,
your being, your energy;
Run, get closer to the edge,
your life you must pledge.

Inner Child

Lay back into my thoughts
To wonder and to weep
Rolling around in memories
I could only wish to reap

Losing Passion

Celebrate your new beginnings,
They are plucked from minds too soon.
The fear remains and the end is nigh,
Our bindings find grip and tightly cocoon,
With the world just watching, thief of my cry.

Culture

How could you love me?
We're so different,
Our cultures in a split so deliberate
We couldn't see eye to eye
Even if we wanted to try.

How could you even try?
To go against our nature,
Our upbringings like a glacier
Ready to rip into the side hull
With doubt piling to the tip of our skull.

Why would you even want to?
It was just so much
To meet another culture's touch.
If ever we broke our bond
My tears would simply fill a pond.

Consistent Rumours

The petal falls once
Curling into its lonesome
As the flower grows

Expectations

Maybe it's just the way it is
One would always make the sale
Defeated of course by the majority
Evolution hasn't struck at the irony
Lost behind the competitive scale

Cruel are we humans in nature
Unless we benefit, there was no need
Lavish are those who are recognised
To reach globally is the true prise
Unless of course, fuelled by greed
Really - they'll tell you to reach for the skies
Eventually, they'll just use you to capitalise

Celebrating the End

Once I had dream,
So long ago now it seems,
For my soul once lit up beams

Worry not for I have peace
And my youth will not cease
My love will only increase

We are a burst of colour
Infectious to one another,
Halting in wait to discover

2020

Did you see it?
See how much the world changed?
See how the cultures were revived?
Did you see it?
See how individualism brought colour?
See how the strings were tied?

Did you hear it?
When the voices cried out in anger?
When she was taken in the night?
Did you hear it?
When those you respected lied?
When you were told the truth and didn't believe
it?

Did you feel it?
The emptiness when they walked away?
The four walls trapping you inside?
Did you feel it?
The kiss you felt so long ago?
The heavy drops of the rain outside?

Did you taste it?
The flavours of your last family meal?
The regret as settling in your bowels?

Did you taste it?
The last lollipop you had?
The last drink you shared?

Did you smell it?
The last time you turned fresh soil?
The last roast in the oven?
Did you smell it?
The cinnamon lingering on your coffee?
The scent of the world lasting on the breeze?

Investing into the People

Extract yourself from the past
Reach instead for desire
And shame you,
Curse you, I will not

Fuel yourself at last
Loyalty, a bond not for hire
Elevates with silent clues
Stars long sought

Blossoming Ideas

The moonflower blossoms
only for a night
only under the light

A beauty for a moment
With no time for obsessing
For it is merely a blessing

Ivory petals that slowly curl
They close by morning
only to continue ever evolving

Anxiety

Trust the rule of three
For not more a chance
Will open to thee

Science VS Opinion

We continue to sow
With all the hopes to grow
Expectant and alert
Our eye on the 'morrow

Lost Ties

Blossom and stand tall
My dear red spider lily
For I will not fall

A Fleeting Memory

Please don't forget me,
I won't be gone long,
There's just a whole world to see.

It's quite a large fee,
To find where I belong -
I promise, I'm not trying to flee.

You may disagree,
May think I'm in the wrong…
But truly, I am free.

Don't forget me my sweet,
For I am not gone,
My adventure is now complete.

I know you feel defeat,
For the curtains have drawn,
But, please, I wish you would eat.

I am by your seat,
With you until dawn -
My love, I will do so on repeat.

To Be Blind; To Be Seen

Oh, little sparrow,
you were hit by an arrow.
Try not to have a fright
for now you have no flight.

Chirp as you may,
young bird you are affray.
Heal and before long
you'll be grown big and strong.

Find comfort not in my nest
for it is only a temporary rest,
soon you'll start your search
and find your very own perch.

Fly away and you'll be free
in your own eye you will see
a world with endless skies,
something I wish for my own eyes.

Emptiness

Look above and fly
Escape from the last tie
And away from the last lie

Down you arm hold
A statement called bold
A line to your heart foretold

Hold true as your right
Give not into fright
Sanity may take flight

The world, it is profound
Although not completely sound
You will find your way around

Swim towards the deep
And find yourself some sleep
The emptiness you will reap

Colour

Brown, crispy leaves, falling to be crunched;
The warmth ebbs away, making way for the
cold.
Out go any possibilities of a summer floral
brunch,
The nights grow longer, casting a blue so bold.

With the trees now bare, colours begin to fade.
The winds pick up and frost lines their lips.
Huddle together and bask in romance crocheted.
Prepare to blossom as the hues begin to eclipse.

The trees begin to bud, dotted with green
And the air becomes perfumed with florals.
Hope and excitement hovers and settles like
steam.
The day stretches its wake as colours return to
corals.

Like umbrellas of shade the trees stood tall
With heat reddening cheeks, sweat dripped its
trail
For now was the moment to climb or to fall.
To never fail, to never try, in age will make you
frail.